Festival of Light
Deepavali Legends from around India

As told by Radhika Sekar

Illustrated by Katherine E. Allen · Designed by David Badour · Edited by Sylvia Pollard

Kaleidoscope Books

Vakils, Feffer & Simons Pvt. Ltd. Mumbai, India

Festival of Light: Deepavali Legends from around India

Radhika Sekar

Ottawa, Canada

www.radhikasekar.com

Illustrated by Katherine E. Allen

Ottawa, Canada

www.embos.ca

Designed by David Badour

Ottawa, Canada

www.badour.ca

Edited by Pollard Editing

Ottawa, Canada

www.pollardediting.com

A Kaleidoscope Book

Published by Vakils, Feffer & Simons Pvt. Ltd.

Mumbai, India

Printed and bound in India

For orders in Canada, contact: kaleidoscopebooks@rogers.com

ISBN: 81-87111-70-4

To
My father, who told me most of these stories
My mother, who celebrated them
Maya and Sonia, for their valuable feedback
And
To my grandson, Maverick—a part of his cultural legacy

About These Stories

Deepavali (or Divali), a Sanskrit word that means "row of lights," is a popular Hindu festival celebrated by all Hindus, irrespective of sect or caste.

It occurs in the Hindu calendar month of *Kartika* (October–November) around the fall equinox when the sun rises exactly in the east and sets exactly in the west. Day and night are of equal duration and in the northern hemisphere the sun is at its lowest elevation. Since Hindu calendars are based on lunisolar calculations, the date varies from year to year. Celebrations begin on the eve of the new moon in the bright half of the month of Kartika, which is called *Naraka Ekadasi*.

Deepavali traditionally marks the end of the fiscal year when accounts are tallied, debts repaid, and employees receive their bonuses. People buy new clothes, distribute sweets, and visit elders to receive their blessings for the coming year.

In southern India, the ritual of *Ganga snanam* (Ganga bath) is customary. Drops of water from the holy river Ganga, gathered and stored in little copper vessels, are added to bath water, which thus sanctified, is believed to cleanse one's sins and omissions of the past year.

Lakshmi—the goddess of wealth—is worshipped on the day after Deepavali; while in northern India, people gamble into the night in the hope of attracting good fortune.

There are several legends that explain the origins of Deepavali. These vary from region to region and sect to sect. The common thread that runs through all of these legends, however, is the triumph of good over bad and the anticipation of prosperity in the coming fiscal year.

It has been the experience of several young mothers that the children of today are upset by excessive goriness and violence—a positive sign indicating that we are producing a more sensitive generation. As with my previous title, *Lord of Beginnings,* I have used the storyteller's prerogative and made subtle changes to minimize the violence in these stories.

Contents

The Stories

Word List

Naraka's Defeat

There lived, in ancient times, an *asura* named Naraka who obtained a boon from the great god Brahma, granting him power over males of all classes—asura, *deva*, and *manusha* (man). Strengthened by this boon, Naraka unleashed a reign of terror on the world, pillaging and looting in all three realms, even conquering *Devaloka* and expelling its ruler, Lord Indra, the King of Devas.

Humiliated by his defeat, Indra rushed—accompanied by his devas—to appeal to the great god Vishnu for help.

At the time, Vishnu was living on earth as Krishna—the King of Dwarka. He was reclining on his throne with his queen, Satyabhama, when Indra burst into the great hall of his palace.

"What is it?" cried Krishna, rising in alarm when he saw Indra's worried face. "Has some disaster befallen you?"

"O great Protector," Indra began breathlessly. "Naraka has conquered my kingdom and expelled all the devas. We now have nowhere to go. What's more, he pillages and plunders at will and harasses everyone. No one can stop him. He is invincible. You must help us."

Krishna's eyes narrowed in displeasure. "Yes," he agreed, "Naraka must be stopped. But it will be difficult. Nevertheless, I will try."

He called for his chariot, then, turning to his queen, who was trained in warfare, said, "Dear Queen, you are skilled in combat. Won't you, therefore, come with me and drive my chariot?"

Pleased that her skills were recognized, the queen willingly agreed to accompany Krishna.

Gathering up his weapons, and with Queen Satyabhama at the helm of his chariot that was pulled by five fine horses, Krishna set off to Naraka's kingdom.

It was the fourteenth day of Kartika, the night of the new moon. Surya, the sun, was at his lowest point on the horizon, and Chandra, the moon, was but a sliver in the sky. The night loomed dark and long and the wind howled menacingly as the queen skilfully steered the chariot on its course.

Finally they arrived at a valley that lay between two tall mountains. The queen steered the chariot through the narrow pass, when suddenly, from out of nowhere emerged a giant boulder that fell with a thud, right in the middle of their path! The five fine horses neighed uneasily as they swerved to avoid it.

"This is Naraka's trickery!" said Krishna, knitting his eyebrows in a frown. Raising his mighty club high above his shoulders, he dealt a crushing blow and the boulder shattered into a thousand pieces!

The way was now cleared and they resumed their journey. The queen skilfully drove the chariot on towards Naraka's kingdom.

Soon, Naraka's fortress loomed in the darkness like a murky shadow. They approached it cautiously, but as they neared, suddenly, from out of nowhere, a barrage of weapons came hurtling towards them! Clubs, spears, swords, arrows, and all kinds of sharp missiles! The five fine horses neighed uneasily as they swerved and darted to avoid them.

"More of Naraka's magic!" declared Krishna impatiently. Picking up his bow, he sent forth a succession of arrows, each with a mighty twang. They flew through the air with lightening speed and split the weapons, every single one, into a thousand pieces!

The way now clear, the queen skilfully drove the chariot on.

Soon they arrived at the gates of the fortress, which even up close was cast in sinister shadows. As they came near, suddenly, the mighty gates burst open and an army of asuras—each more grue-some than the next—came storming out.

Howling savagely as they flung their spears, they set upon the chariot. The five fine horses neighed uneasily as they swerved, darted, and dashed, here and there, to avoid their weapons.

"Naraka's army of asuras!" scoffed Krishna. Fearlessly he fought them off with his sword until they ran away— every last one of them—in a thousand directions!

The way now clear, the queen skilfully steered the chariot on, passing through the gates, right up to the massive doors of Naraka's fortress, which still loomed like a murky shadow in the darkness.

"Naraka!" roared Krishna. "Enough of your trickery. Come out and face me!"

The massive doors of the dreary fortress creaked open and out rode Naraka, atop his elephant. He was angry and arrogant.

"Fool!" he called out. "Don't you know that I have power over all males?"

With an evil laugh, eyes flashing hate, he flung his spear at Krishna with all his might. It struck his shoulder and Krishna, the King of Dwarka, slumped to the chariot floor.

"Ha, ha, ha!" laughed Naraka fiendishly. "That was too easy."

But Queen Satyabhama, who was skilled in warfare, snatched up Krishna's bow and called out, "Naraka, your boon grants you power over all *males*. But dare you fight a woman?"

Taken aback by the challenge, Naraka turned to face the queen. His nostrils flaring and lips curling in a scornful sneer, he snorted arrogantly. "You! What can you do? I'll squash you like a bug!"

The brave queen stood her ground and with careful aim sent her arrows flying. Like lightening, they sped through the air, finding their mark before Naraka could even string his bow!

"A-H-U-G-G-O-O-O-H!" roared the mighty Naraka, his scream rent the sky as he fell to the ground with a thud. Naraka was defeated, for asuras lose their powers when they fall to the ground.

Krishna, who was, of course, none other than the great god Vishnu and only pretending to be wounded, sat up and cheered the queen's bravery.

"The mighty Naraka is felled at last!" Lord Indra and the devas chorused. Flowers fell from the sky, as Indra and the devas, and all the creatures of the world, came out to celebrate the end of Naraka's tyranny. They distributed sweets, set off fireworks, and lit lamps to brighten the path for Krishna and the brave queen as they set off to return through the dark night.

And, to this day, Hindus in southern India remember Queen Satyabhama's victory over the wicked Naraka by joyfully lighting lamps to brighten this, the darkest night of the year.

Churning of the Ocean

Once, in ancient times, the asuras became very strong, while the devas remained weak. Concerned for the balance of power, Lord Indra, the King of Devas, sought out the great god Vishnu.

"O great Vishnu, Protector of Peace and Harmony," chorused Indra and his delegation of thirty-three thousand devas. "The asuras grow more powerful by the day, while we devas remain weak. Tell us, O Wise One, how we may increase our strength so that we can stand against them."

Vishnu looked down upon them from his serpent throne. Stroking his chin thoughtfully, he replied in a booming voice, "Indra, devas, listen carefully to what I say. Deep in a cavern, under the bottomless ocean, lies buried a golden pot filled with *amrita*—the elixir of immortality. Those who drink of it will gain great strength and immortality. Raise it and use it as you will."

"How do we raise it?" asked the bewildered devas.

"By churning the ocean, of course," replied Vishnu.

"We are not strong enough," lamented the devas.

"Then you must ask the asuras to help you," retorted Vishnu, impatiently.

"But will they not want a share of the potion?" asked the devas.

"I will make sure they do not get any," assured Vishnu, with a mischievous twinkle in his eyes.

Indra and his delegation then approached Lord Bali, the King of Asuras. They told him about the pot of amrita at the bottom of the ocean.

"But we are not strong enough to churn the ocean and raise it by ourselves," they admitted. "We need your help."

After much haggling, Bali and his asuras agreed to help them—as long as they received their fair share of the potion. Peace was declared, and devas and asuras set off to churn the bottomless ocean together.

It was the fifteenth day of the bright half of Kartika, the night of the new moon. Surya was at his lowest point on the horizon, and Chandra was but a sliver in the sky. The night loomed dark and long.

Using the highest mountain as a pole, and the longest serpent as a rope, devas and asuras began churning the ocean. They churned with great gusto and as they churned fish, sharks, and even the whales in the ocean were tossed up and down.

At last, from out of the waters, surfaced a smouldering cauldron of vile blue liquid.

"Surely this cannot be the amrita?" wondered devas and asuras alike. "But who is to test it?"

Just then the great god Shiva happened by and he gamesomely offered to taste it. Lifting the smouldering cauldron to his lips, he took a mighty swig.

But the goddess Parvati, afraid for her husband, tightly grasped his neck so that the fluid stayed at his throat. The blue liquid, which was indeed noxious, stained Shiva's neck, so that from thereon he became known as Nilakantha—the Blue-Necked One!

A tiny drop of poison fell to the ground and was lapped up by snakes, scorpions, and other creepy-crawly creatures that have venomous fangs.

The asuras and devas then returned to their task and began churning the ocean once more. Again, they churned with great gusto and as they churned the ocean swirled and swished, tossing the fish, sharks, and even the whales of the ocean up and down.

At last, from out of the water emerged a pink lotus, upon which sat a radiant *devi*, a goddess. Dressed in silks of green and gold, jewels gleaming at her neck and wrists, she held a garland of fragrant flowers in her hands. Gold coins fell from her palms and her anklets tinkled as she moved.

Indra hurried to fetch a throne for her to sit upon and Bali brought a parasol to shield her. Rivers swelled in their banks, cows yielded more milk, and Mother Earth brought forth a bountiful harvest that year.

With a sweet smile hovering on her lips, the devi looked around shyly for a husband. Spotting the great god Vishnu, so strong and handsome, she placed the garland around his neck. Thus, married to Vishnu, she became Lakshmi, the Goddess of Prosperity.

People came to worship the goddess and seek her blessings for the coming year. They lit lamps to brighten the dark night and distributed sweets and other delicacies. There was much feasting and rejoicing.

The devas and asuras returned to their task of churning the ocean once more. They churned with great gusto and as they churned, the oceans swirled and swished, tossing fish, sharks, and even the whales of the ocean up and down.

At last, from out of the waters emerged a radiant being bearing a golden pot. "I am Dattatreya, the Lord of Good Health and Medicine," he announced. "Here is the amrita that you seek. Those who drink it will gain strength and immortality."

There was a great cheer as the devas and asuras realized that their task was over. Both Lords Indra and Bali stepped forward to take the pot.

"As it was our idea, we will drink of it first," said Indra, tugging it to the right.

"Without us, you would not have had the strength to churn the ocean," retorted Bali, tugging it to the left. "Give it to us first."

And so it went, back and forth, right and left. Tempers flared and it almost came to blows, when suddenly! ...

Suddenly, from out of nowhere, appeared a beautiful maiden such as they had never seen! Her dark eyes were like blue lotuses and her air of mystery enchanted devas and asuras alike.

Smiling sweetly, she took the pot from them. "Silly men, why quarrel over this?" she scolded playfully. "Sit down and I will serve it equally amongst you."

Meekly they sat down, devas facing north and asuras facing south, as the beautiful maiden danced between them. Flirting outrageously with the asuras, she distracted them while she slyly served the amrita to the devas. Soon, all the devas had received the magic potion and there was not a drop left for the asuras.

The beautiful maiden then threw down the pot and, laughing scornfully, vanished as suddenly as she had appeared.

The spell was broken and the asuras realized that they had been tricked! There was no potion left for them.

But two asuras, called Rahu and Ketu, realizing that they were being tricked, had sat down amongst the devas. Thus, they had received a share of the amrita and were now immortal.

When the great god Vishnu found out about them, he banished them to the sky, where they could do the least mischief. There they became shadows, destined to chase the sun and moon on their orbits through eternity. But, every now and then, the crafty pair play catch-up with Surya and eclipse him, thus plunging the sky into darkness.

As for the rest, the asuras rushed for their weapons and peace was ended. But, having drunk the potion of immortality, the devas were now an even match for the asuras and the balance of power was restored.

However, to this day, Hindus celebrate the birth of the goddess Lakshmi from the bottomless ocean, and her marriage to Vishnu, on this darkest night of the year, by lighting Deepavali—row of lights.

On the next day, they worship Lakshmi, the Goddess of Wealth and Prosperity, to seek her blessings for the coming year. Some also worship the golden Dattatreya, the Lord of Medicine, for bringing forth the pot of amrita, and pray for good health and a long life.

The Slaying of Ravana and Return of Prince Rama

There lived in ancient times a mighty *rakshasa*—a most fearsome asura—named Ravana who, strengthened by a boon granted to him by the great god Brahma, unleashed a reign of terror on the world.

Unable to bear his cruelty, the devas approached the great god Vishnu for help.

"O great Vishnu," they cried. "Ravana is terrorizing the world, plundering and looting at will. Because Lord Brahma granted him power over all devas and asuras, we are helpless against him. You must help put a stop to him."

Vishnu's eyes narrowed as he listened intently. "You say that devas and asuras are helpless against him," he observed. "What about men and animals?"

"There was no mention of them in the boon," replied the devas. "But," they added scornfully, "men are such weak creatures. They possess neither strength nor supernatural powers. How can they stand up to Ravana?"

"H'm," murmured Vishnu, stroking his chin thoughtfully. "We'll see about that. Tell me, is there anyone on earth at this moment praying for a son?"

"Yes," replied the devas. "King Dasaratha of Ayodhya is at this very minute performing a huge sacrifice for an heir."

"*Thatha stu!* Let his wish be granted," declared Vishnu, with a mysterious twinkle in his eyes.

Dasaratha was a brave and honourable king and his people were happy and prosperous. As was the custom in those days, he had three beautiful queens, but, to his bitter disappointment, no heirs. He decided, therefore, to perform a *homa*—a fire sacrifice to please the gods.

Building a great fire, Dasaratha poured ghee and other offerings into it while a thousand priests chanted holy mantras invoking the devas. The best of his cattle were sacrificed and gifts of land, cattle, fine clothes, and gold were distributed to the deserving.

Towards the end of the sacrifice, a radiant being emerged from the fire. He held out a golden bowl and, addressing the king in a booming voice, said, "Great King, the devas are pleased with your sacrifice and send you their blessings. Give this *payasam* to your queens and they will bear you noble sons."

Soon thereafter, to Dasaratha's delight, each of his queens became with child and, in due course, delivered handsome sons. The eldest of the princes, named Rama, was especially gifted with beauty, strength, and dignity.

When Rama came of age, he won the hand of the beautiful Princess Sita of Mithila. Dasaratha, who had become old and weary, decided that the time had come for him to retire and to make Rama king. Everyone rejoiced, for Prince Rama was greatly loved.

Everyone, that is, except for Kaikeyi, Dasaratha's youngest and favourite queen, who wished her own son, Bharatha, to rule. Reminding Dasaratha of two wishes he had granted her in the past, she demanded that Rama be banished to the forest for thirteen years and that Bharatha be made king in his place.

Upon hearing her demands, the old king collapsed in grief. But Prince Rama took the news with dignity. "Dear Queen," he said, bowing solemnly. "I will honour my father's promises."

Discarding his royal robes, Rama donned the plain attire of a woodsman and left for the forest. The beautiful Sita and his brother, Lakshmana, from whom Rama was inseparable, went with him.

In the forest the three built a small hut to live in and settled into a simple life. Rama and Lakshmana hunted by day, while Sita collected berries and cooked whatever they brought home. They made friends with the many sages and woodsmen who also lived in the forest and the years passed happily.

Meanwhile, the wicked Ravana was growing more powerful day by day. He threatened both asuras and devas, and even stole the winged chariot that belonged to Kubera, the Lord of Riches! Moreover, under his leadership, all the other rakshasas also became unruly and troublesome.

Hearing of Sita's great beauty, Ravana decided that he must have her for his bride. He commanded his uncle, Maricha, to disguise himself as a beautiful spotted golden deer and lure Rama and Lakshmana away from the hut. Then, disguised as a poor old man, Ravana went to the hut begging for alms.

When the kind-hearted Sita brought out a bowl of rice for him, he turned back into the ten-headed rakshasa and carried her off in Kubera's winged chariot.

As Ravana sped away with Sita to his kingdom of Lanka, Jatayu, the King of Birds, tried to stop him. But Ravana merely laughed wickedly and chopped off his wings.

When Rama and Lakshmana returned, they searched high and low for Sita. Finally they came upon Jatayu, lying wounded on the ground.

"Rama, Lakshmana," gasped Jatayu hoarsely. "Ravana tricked you with the spotted golden deer. He has carried Sita away to Lanka in a winged chariot. I could not save her."

The princes were devastated. "We must rescue her!" cried Rama unhappily.

"But how?" asked Lakshmana. "Ravana is all-powerful and has a large army of gruesome rakshasas. Also, because of Lord Brahma's boon, he is stronger than the devas and asuras. How can we fight him?"

"We must, at least, try," said Rama. "Poor Sita will be so sad and frightened."

Just then, a *vanara* called Hanuman came by and wondered who the handsome princes were.

"Who are you?" he asked. "And why are you so sad?"

Rama explained how Ravana had tricked them and carried away Sita. "She must be rescued, but alas, we have no army. How can we fight the mighty Ravana?"

Calling all the monkeys of the forest together, Hanuman replied, "Don't be discouraged, dear Prince. We will help you. Our monkey army will gather stones and make a bridge across the sea to Lanka."

And so, Hanuman and his monkey army began building a bridge. All the animals of the forest came out to help, even the little chipmunks. Rama stroked them lovingly and to this day they proudly bear the marks of his fingers on their backs.

Seven times Surya rose in the east and sank in the west and on the eighth day, the bridge was complete. It was the fifteenth day of Kartika and the night of the new moon. Surya was at his lowest point on the horizon, and Chandra was but a sliver in the sky. Night loomed dark and long. Followed by the monkey army, Rama and Lakshmana crossed the bridge into Lanka.

Thousands and thousands of rakshasas came out to meet them, howling savagely and hurling spears. The monkeys fought fiercely and valiantly alongside Rama and Lakshmana.

At last Ravana came out of his castle. Beating his chest and shaking his ten heads threateningly, he gave a mighty roar. He was a scary sight!

"Have you come to fight me, Rama?" he mocked with a wicked laugh. "Don't you know that neither deva nor asura can overpower me? How dare you, a mere man and a pack of monkeys challenge me?"

But Rama stood his ground fearlessly. Stringing his bow, he let fly an arrow with a mighty twang! It whizzed through the air like lightening and severed one of Ravana's heads. However, no sooner did the head fall to the ground than another grew in its place!

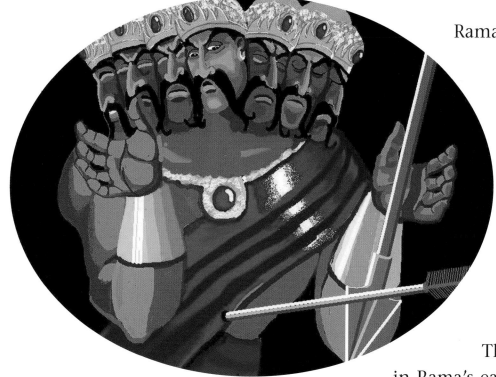

Rama sent another arrow …

And then another …

And another …

But each time a head was severed, another grew back on.

Ravana's mocking laughter grew louder and louder until it shook the earth and rent the sky.

"Ha, ha, ha! Is this all you can do?"

Then Hanuman stepped up and whispered in Rama's ear, "The seat of his power lies in his belly. Aim your arrows there."

With lightening speed, Rama's arrow sped through the air and found its mark before Ravana could lift his club.

"A-H-U-G-G-G-O-O-O-O-H!" roared the mighty Ravana. His scream rent the sky as he fell to the ground with a thud. Ravana was defeated, for rakshasas, like asuras, lose their magic powers once they fall to the ground.

When they saw their leader fall, the rakshasa army fled in panic. The monkey army cheered as they realized that the battle was over. Flowers fell from the sky as devas gathered to rejoice. "The mighty Ravana was defeated by a 'mere' man and an army of monkeys!" they chorused.

Sita came out of the castle, her gentle face full of love. Greeting her joyfully, Rama declared, "Our period of exile is over today. We will return home to Ayodhya."

Kubera, the Lord of Riches, offered them his winged chariot to carry them back home. Hanuman went with them.

The people of Ayodhya were eagerly awaiting their rightful king's return. Even Rama's brother, Bharatha, was overjoyed, for he, too, wanted Rama to be king and had merely been looking after Ayodhya until his return. They lit rows and rows of lamps to brighten the dark night and greet the royal couple. Rama's coronation was celebrated by a burst of fireworks and a great feast. Fine clothes and sweets were distributed to everyone.

And, to this day, many Hindus celebrate the defeat of Ravana and the return of Rama from exile by lighting lamps on this darkest night of the year!

The Goddess Who Would Not Stop Dancing

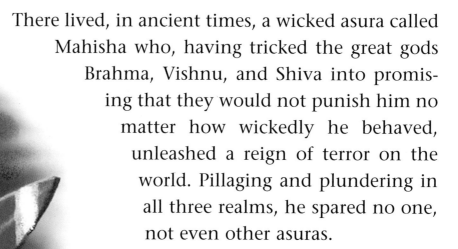

There lived, in ancient times, a wicked asura called Mahisha who, having tricked the great gods Brahma, Vishnu, and Shiva into promising that they would not punish him no matter how wickedly he behaved, unleashed a reign of terror on the world. Pillaging and plundering in all three realms, he spared no one, not even other asuras.

Unable to bear his tyranny, the devas, asuras, and men sought the advice of the three great gods.

"Alas," sighed Brahma the Creator, shaking his head sadly, "there is nothing we can do, for we promised never to check up on him."

"Then what is to become of the world?" cried the devas anxiously.

"We will all be destroyed!" wailed the men in despair.

"There must be a way to stop him!" shrieked the asuras heatedly.

The great gods sat pondering the problem for awhile.

Finally, Shiva said, with a clever smile, "It is true that we gods cannot interfere in this matter. However, our goddesses made no such promise. Let us, therefore, ask our wives—Parvati, Lakshmi, and Saraswati—to subdue the cruel Mahisha."

"Mahisha is very strong," observed Parvati, when she considered the problem. "But we could overcome him, if we combined our strength."

Forming a circle, the three goddesses held hands and chanted a holy mantra. The air around them glowed radiantly, enveloping them in a brilliant bright haze. Brighter and brighter did it become until, with a sudden flash, there emerged from the haze a single goddess—tall as a coconut tree and powerful as the wind. Mounted on a tiger, she had ten arms, each holding a weapon of war, and wore a garland of skulls around her neck. All who saw her cringed in fear, for she was very fierce indeed!

"We will call her Mahadevi—the great goddess," said Shiva.

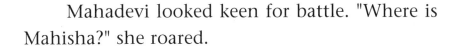

Mahadevi looked keen for battle. "Where is Mahisha?" she roared.

"Here I am," called Mahisha from atop his elephant. He, too, was eager to fight.

Fearlessly Mahadevi galloped towards him, looking majestic astride her tiger.

With his magic powers, Mahisha conjured up a dust storm that screened him from her sight.

But, ordering the clouds to gather, Mahadevi made it rain, which settled the dust.

Mahisha set fire to forests. Mahadevi sent hurricane winds to put out the fire.

Mahisha pounded the earth and it quaked and split into deep crevices. Mahadevi caused the volcanoes to erupt and the hot lava filled the cracks and made the earth whole again.

Thus, the battle raged for nine days and nine nights. Mahisha used every magic trick in his power, but the goddess successfully countered every one of them.

On the tenth day, Mahisha grew weary. He had no more tricks left and had to face the goddess directly. He charged towards her on his trumpeting elephant. But before he could even use his weapon, Mahadevi flung her lance at him with lightening speed and knocked him off his elephant!

"A-H-U-G-G-G-O-O-O-H!" roared the mighty Mahisha. His scream rent the sky as he fell with a thud! The battle was over, for asuras lose their magic powers once they fall to the ground.

"*Vijaya!* Victory!" shouted Mahadevi, and the day became known as *Vijaya Dashami*—the tenth day of victory.

"Mahadevi *ki jaya!* Victory to the great goddess!" chorused devas and asuras alike, as flowers fell from the sky and people came out to celebrate.

Mahadevi was ecstatic. She began to dance, brandishing her weapons as she flailed her arms.

"You can put down your weapons now," suggested Shiva. "Mahisha has been destroyed."

But Mahadevi did not hear him. She kept on dancing.

Mother Earth groaned as Mahadevi stamped her feet in a frenzy.

Sparks flew from her eyes, clouds gathered, and thunder and lightening rent the sky. Rain came down in torrents.

Alarmed by the goddess's frenzy, Surya hid behind the clouds and the world became dreary.

"Her dancing is causing havoc!" cried the devas.

"The world will be destroyed if she does not stop dancing!" wailed the people.

"Gods, do something!" hollered the asuras.

But no one, not even Shiva, who is Lord of the Dance, could stop Mahadevi from dancing on and on and on.

The moon waxed and waned twice and finally, on the fifteenth day of Kartika, she showed signs of calming down.

"Quick!" urged Shiva. "Prepare a feast in her honour."

Lamps were lit to brighten the night and joyful songs, praising the goddess's victory were sung. A great feast was prepared, and people bought new clothes and distributed sweets in her honour.

When Mahadevi saw the festivities she smiled happily and slowed down."Is this for me?" she asked. Tranquility was restored.

To this day, Hindus in Bengal celebrate Deepavali as the day the goddess stopped dancing after her battle with Mahishasura.

Three Steps of Land

Long ago, in ancient times, there lived a great king called Bali who, although he was an asura, was generous, honourable, and just.

One day, Bali decided to perform a great homa to call up the great god Brahma, Creator of the World. Building a great fire, he poured ghee and other offerings into it while a thousand priests chanted holy mantras. The best of his cattle were sacrificed and gifts of land, cattle, fine clothes, and gold were distributed to all.

The devas, however, were greatly alarmed by Bali's devotion. "What if Lord Brahma grants him a boon that will make him invincible?" they worried. "He must be stopped before he can cause harm."

Rushing to Vaikunta, where the great god Vishnu lives, they appealed for his help.

"O great Protector of the World," they cried, addressing Vishnu. "King Bali is performing a huge homa to call up the great god Brahma. He must be stopped before Brahma grants him a boon. Remember the trouble we had with Naraka, Ravana, and Mahisha?"

"Yes, indeed, I do," replied Vishnu gravely, looking down at them from his serpent throne. "But isn't Bali a kind and just king?"

"Yes," replied the devas. "Also very generous. But power may go to his head and make him cruel."

"You are right," agreed Vishnu. "He must be stopped before he can cause trouble."

Meanwhile, King Bali was very pleased at the way his sacrifice was going. He had fed a thousand priests, bestowed lands to ten thousand noblemen, rewarded twenty thousand artisans, and clothed thirty thousand peasants. Orphans had been found homes, and the poor and sick had been cared for.

"Surely Lord Brahma must be pleased," Bali said to himself. "It's only a matter of time before he appears to reward me."

Just then, a small dwarf entered the sacrificial hall. "O great King," said the dwarf. "I see that you are giving away gifts. May I, too, have a gift?"

"Of course," replied Bali generously.

"No one is to be turned away. Ask for anything and it is yours."

"All I want is a small piece of land," said the dwarf, bowing low. "Just three steps will do."

"Is that all?" Bali was puzzled. The dwarf had such tiny legs. "You could ask for much more. A large estate, food, clothing, riches, perhaps even a beautiful bride."

"No, no," said the dwarf, shaking his head. "I have no need of such things. Just three steps will do."

"*Thatha stu!* So be it!" pronounced King Bali, waving his hand generously. "Take your three steps, Dwarf."

The dwarf then stretched as tall as he could and took his first step. To everyone's surprise, it covered the whole earth!

Stretching tall once more, the little dwarf took his second step. To Bali's alarm, it covered the whole sky!

Stretching once more, the little dwarf raised his leg to take his third step. But there was nowhere to place it. He had already covered the whole world!

"You promised me three steps," he said. "Where should I place my foot now?"

Realizing that the dwarf was none other than the great god Vishnu, Bali knelt to the ground and bowed his head. "I always fulfill my promises," he declared gravely. "I promised you three steps and three steps you shall have. Place the third on my head, O Lord."

The dwarf then placed his foot on Bali's head and pushed him deep into the underworld.

Petals fell from the sky as devas came out to rejoice.

But the people—asuras and humans—of Bali's kingdom were not happy, for they loved their generous king. Vishnu, too, felt sorry for him, for, after all, he was good and kind.

"Bali, you are a good king and your people love you. Therefore, you may return to visit them once a year," he announced.

And thus, once a year, on the sixteenth day of Kartika—the second day of Deepavali—when the day is short and the night is long, Bali returns to visit his people, who greet him with great rejoicing.

The Humbling of Indra

Vrindavan is a little village in Rajasthan, in northwestern India. Its people were mostly farmers and shepherds who grazed their cattle on the lush slopes of the nearby Govardhana hill. Each year, the villagers held a great homa in honour of Indra, the Lord of Rain, to thank him for the monsoons. It was held on the sixteenth day of Kartika, during the Deepavali celebrations. Ghee and other offerings were poured into the sacred fire, while priests chanted holy mantras. Cattle were sacrificed, followed by a great feast to which even passersby were welcomed.

Once, unknown to the villagers, the great god Vishnu was living amongst them in his eighth incarnation, as the cowherd, Krishna. He was upset by the slaughter of the cows.

"How can sacrificing these gentle, selfless creatures effect the fall of rain?" he demanded. "How is it beneficial at all? Let us instead honour someone who looks after our welfare, like the Govardhana mountain. This mountain blocks the rain-bearing clouds for our fields and provides grazing grounds for our cattle."

The farmers saw sense in his arguments and decided not to sacrifice any more cattle.

Indra, however, was infuriated when he heard about their decision. "How dare they?!" he roared. "Don't they know how powerful I am?"

With a crash of thunder and a flash of lightening, he sent down torrential rains to drown the residents of Vrindavan.

It rained for days ...

Weeks ...

Fields were submerged ...

Rivers overflowed ...

The village was flooded!

"What shall we do?" cried the farmers. "Our crops are ruined and our homes are flooded and we may all be drowned! This is Krishna's fault."

Suddenly the earth rumbled and shook. Fearing an earthquake, the villagers ran here and there looking for shelter. Then, just as suddenly, the rumbling stopped and, to their surprise, the Govardhana hill ... began rising!

Up it rose, higher and higher, until it soared above them. Then, to their further amazement, they saw that it was being held overhead by Krishna, the cowherd, like a giant umbrella. He was balancing it on one finger!

"Come, hurry and take shelter," he invited them, with a mischievous grin. "It's warm and dry under here."

Seeing that he was outdone, Indra withdrew the rain and clouds. Bowing to Krishna— whom, he realized, was none other than the great god Vishnu—he begged for mercy.

"Shame on you, Indra," scolded Krishna sternly. "Power corrupted you, so from hereinafter you will no longer be honoured. Now, go and use your powers wisely."

The farmers were overjoyed. "Let us hold a feast to honour Krishna's feat," they said joyfully.

And, to this day, people celebrate Krishna's feat during the Deepavali festival by holding a special *puja*. As for Indra, he is honoured no more, because he misused his powers.

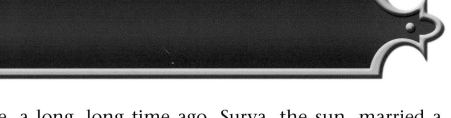

A Brother's Gift

Once, a long, long time ago, Surya, the sun, married a beautiful princess, Samjna, who bore him twins. They were named Yama and Yami. However, unable to bear the heat of her husband's brilliance, the princess ran away, leaving her shadow, Chhaya, behind in her place.

Chhaya turned out to be a cruel stepmother and was very unkind to the twins. When her own children were born, she made their father banish the twins from the sky. Yami fell to earth and became the river Yamuna, while Yama went to the underworld and became the King of Death!

Years passed. Yami married a handsome prince and was content and happy. But she missed her brother and yearned to see him.

Yama, too, missed his sister and decided one day to visit her.

Overjoyed by news of her brother's visit, Yami prepared a great feast in his honour. It was two days into Deepavali, so her home was already decorated with pretty lamps. She lovingly prepared a feast, including all the sweets and delicacies that her brother loved. Her husband, the handsome prince, rejoiced to see her so happy.

Yama, too, was delighted by his sister's loving welcome, and brother and sister spent a pleasant evening in each other's company.

When it was time for Yama to return to his kingdom in the underworld, he turned to his sister and said, "Dear Yami, you have welcomed me so lovingly. But I did not bring you a gift. Ask, therefore, for something and it will be yours."

"Your visit is gift enough," replied Yami lovingly. "I have no need of anything else."

But Yama was persistent. "You must let me give you a gift," he insisted.

"Very well," agreed Yami, taking a moment to think. "I ask that all brothers should remember their sisters on this day and visit them if they can, and that, on this day, all sisters should pray for the happiness of their brothers."

"*Thatha stu!* So be it!" proclaimed Yama, the King of Death, adding, "And I grant all brothers who give their sisters a loving gift on this day a long and healthy life!"

So, to all you brothers out there: Be sure to remember your sisters on this day and give them loving gifts—be they ever so small.

And, to all sisters: You, too, must think of your brothers and pray for their well-being on this special day.

Word List

amrita. A drink of immortality, elixir, or magic potion.

asura, deva, and *manusha.* There are three types of beings in Hindu stories:

  • *Asuras* are ogre-like beings that may be bad or good. They possess enormous strength and magical powers, but are rather crude and easily corrupted by power.

  • *Devas* are gods or radiant beings who inhabit the skies and mountaintops, rivers, and other sacred areas. They use their powers for good, but occasionally may also need checking—as in the story "The Humbling of Indra." There are 33,000 devas in the Hindu pantheon.

   Brahma, Vishnu, and *Shiva* are the great gods. They are elevated above the other devas and form what has become known as the Hindu Trinity. Brahma is the creator, Vishnu protects creation, and, when the time comes, Shiva oversees its end. Thus, each of the great gods has a role in the smooth running of the world. It becomes Vishnu's duty to restore the balance of power whenever the asuras become too strong.

   Other devas mentioned, like *Indra* (rain), *Surya* (sun), and *Chandra* (moon), are demigods who represent the constellations or different aspects of nature. Devi is the female of Deva.

All gods have a devi counterpart, the most important ones being: ***Saraswati, Lakshmi,*** and ***Parvati.*** Saraswati is the Goddess of Learning and the wife of Brahma; Lakshmi, the Goddess of Prosperity, is married to Vishnu; and, Parvati is the wife of Shiva, and is the Goddess of Fertility.

In the story "The Goddess Who Would Not Stop Dancing," these three devis merge to form a single powerful goddess who is called ***Mahadevi,*** the Great Goddess.

• ***Manusha*** are earthly beings, that is, humans. They are not as physically strong as the asuras, nor do they possess magic powers, but must rely on virtue and honour to overcome problems.

Devaloka. The kingdom of the devas of which Indra is king.

homa. A fire ritual.

Krishna. The King of Dwarka is the eighth incarnation of Vishnu. It is believed that from time to time the great god Vishnu comes down to earth and takes either a human or anthropomorphic (half human/half animal) form in order to restore the balance of good in the world.

puja. Worship or prayers.

payasam. A pudding made of milk, rice, sugar, and almonds, garnished with saffron.

Rajasthan. A state in the northwestern part of India.

rakshasa. Another class of asura, or ogre-like being.

vanara. Vanaras are mythical beings (half human/half monkey) who have the power of flight.

About the Author

Born in India, Radhika Sekar has lived in Canada since 1974. She holds a PhD in Religious Studies and taught Hinduism at Carleton University. Now a full-time writer, she has published short stories in various anthologies and in 2004 was a winner in the City of Ottawa, Short Story Contest. Having brought up two children in Canada, Radhika realizes the problems of perpetuating heritage traditions in an alien environment. She hopes that this book, and others in the Kaleidoscope Books series, including *Lord of Beginnings—Stories of the Elephant-Headed Deity: Ganesha,* will fill that void and encourage children of all backgrounds and ages to learn more about Hindu culture. Radhika now resides in Ottawa with her husband and is a proud new grandmother.

The next title in her series is: *Stories of Hanuman.*

About the Editor

Sylvia Pollard settled in Ottawa to study music at Carleton University, finishing with a degree in English and Geography. A member of the Editors' Association of Canada, Sylvia has published many articles and reviews on art, literature, and music, and edited countless novels, short stories, and academic manuscripts. Passionate about the arts and aware of the lifelong impact of our most-beloved childhood books, she is honoured to be involved in the Kaleidscope Books series. Sylvia also publishes her own short stories, poems, and songs in her serial chapbook, *Willow,* and teaches guitar.